THE

BUSY PEOPLE'S

DELIGHTFUL

DINNER BOOK

Meatless Recipes by Sharon Elliot

fresh press

To Megan,
　　　　whose spirit is a delight
　　　　　　　　　and
　　　　　　　　　To Grant,
　　　　　　　　　　　with whom so much seems possible.

Published by Fresh Press
　　　　　　774 Allen Court
　　　　　　Palo Alto, California 94303

To order by mail send your name and address
along with a check for $6.70 ($7.06 if you
live in California) to Fresh Press
at the above address.

Library of Congress Number: 83-83025
ISBN: 0-9601398-6-9

Printed by CONSOLIDATED PUBLICATIONS

Revised Edition　January 1984
Cover by Hae Yuon Kim

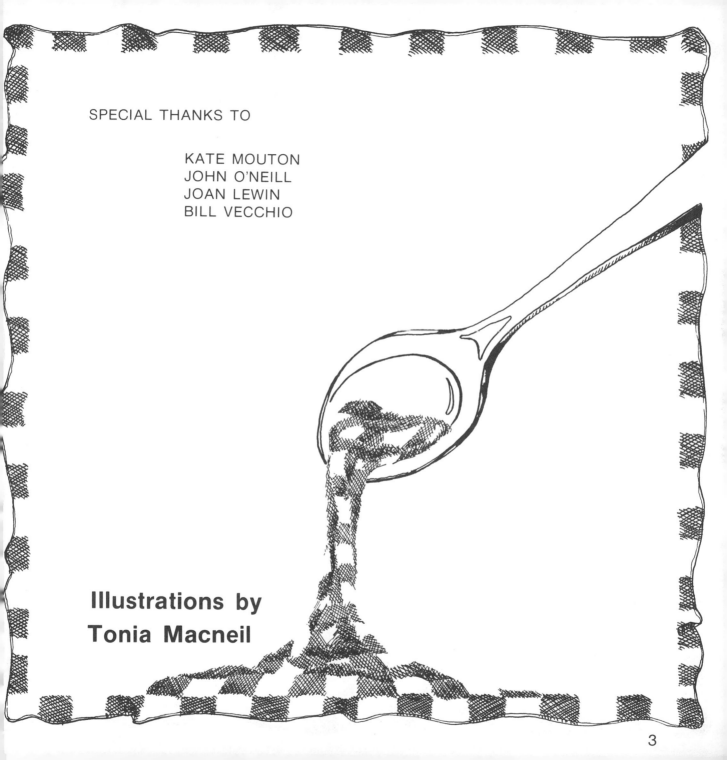

SPECIAL THANKS TO

KATE MOUTON
JOHN O'NEILL
JOAN LEWIN
BILL VECCHIO

**Illustrations by
Tonia Macneil**

CONTENTS

INTRODUCTION

Why a dinner book for busy people? Because many busy people like to spend some time in the kitchen creating tasty, unusual — occasionally even memorable — dinners. Many busy people also appreciate the fact that foods prepared at home can easily be more nutritious and less expensive than restaurant food.

THE DELIGHTFUL DINNER BOOK offers busy people a chance to enjoy cooking without worrying about nutrition, money or time. The fresh, unprocessed (or minimally processed) ingredients called for in DINNER recipes are low in cost and high in nutrients. The amounts of salt, fat and sweetening listed are low and, in most cases, can be reduced further for educated palates.

DINNER is specially formatted to help busy people use time well. Main dish, vegetable and soup recipes are arranged according to preparation time. A recipe near the front of a section takes less time to prepare than those farther on. The recipes themselves are presented in efficient work sections. These sections can be handled easily by a single cook or can be shared among cooks in a cooperative effort. Even making a shopping list from DINNER takes less time because recipe ingredients are printed separately in large type.

Most DINNER recipes are completed in the kitchen. Some are finished at the table. With their casual, low pressure approach, these recipes encourage diners to try unfamiliar foods and/or new combinations. They give everyone the pleasure of creating his own unique meal — one that's just right for his body at that particular time.

Be sure not to nibble away the leftovers at the end of a DINNER meal. One of the rewards of cooking with DINNER is that its good foods can take on a variety of forms. What appears at one night's dinner can star the next day in a breakfast nibble, a luncheon sandwich, a soup, or a salad. Tahini sauces can reappear as salad dressings, dips, or sauces for hot veggies. Mexican and Italian Eggplant are delicious mixed with cottage cheese or ricotta and packed in a luncheon thermos. Try Re-fried Black Beans piled on toast, covered with cheese and broiled for a special "forker" sandwich. Mixed with mayonnaise and extra salt, both Lentil Chili and Leapin' Lentils make delicious sandwich fillings, dips, or spreads.

DINNER recipes are structured with an eye to minimizing clean-up and dishwashing. We hope you enjoy your new found leisure time!

Sharon Elliot

Recipes in this chapter are arranged according to the time required for preparation. If you need an idea one hour before dinner, look at the beginning. As you move through the chapter, recipes take more total time to be readied (although your actual work time may still be short). At the end of the chapter you will find recipes like Jan's Falafel and Surprise Loaf. Don't let their need for overnight planning keep you from trying them!

MAIN DISHES

ABBY'S SANDWICH

Sauté over low heat until clear
  1 LARGE ONION, CHOPPED FINE

In
  2-4 TBS. BUTTER

Add
  ¾-1 TSP. CURRY POWDER
Sauté a moment, then add
  1 LB. MUSHROOMS, CHOPPED
  2 LARGE TASTY APPLES, CHOPPED
  ⅜ TSP. SALT
Sauté, stirring often, for 5-10 minutes—until soft.

Spoon ¼ of the vegetable mixture onto each of
  4 WHOLE GRAIN BREAD SLICES
Cover with
  THINLY SLICED MONTEREY JACK CHEESE
Add
  ALFALFA SPROUTS, TO TASTE
Top each sandwich with another slice of
  WHOLE GRAIN BREAD

Let sit a minute to warm the cheese.
Serves 4.

FAMILY FONDUE

THE DIPPERS

Arrange some or all of the following on platters or individual serving plates
        FRENCH OR SOUR DOUGH BREAD CUBES*
        FIRM TOFU CUBES
        ROUNDS OF CARROTS, ZUCCHINI, AND CROOKNECK SQUASH
        FLOWERETS OF CAULIFLOWER AND BROCCOLI
        JICAMA CUBES
        APPLE CHUNKS
        SMALL MUSHROOMS

THE FONDUE

Mix in a large bowl
        4 CUPS (1 LB.) GRATED CHEDDAR OR JACK CHEESE
        ¼ CUP FLOUR
Set aside.

Heat to simmering in a saucepan or fondue pot
        1¼ CUPS MILK
        ¼ CUP (2 OZ.) CHOPPED GREEN CHILES (OPTIONAL)
Add
        THE CHEESE MIXTURE, a handful at a time, stirring after each
            addition until melted
If desired, the fondue may be thinned by adding a little extra warmed milk.

Set the saucepan or fondue pot over a low heat source at the table.
Pass the dippers!
Serves 4.
See Fall Menu Suggestions (page 121).

*Cinnamon-raisin bread makes delicious dunking when FAMILY FONDUE doesn't have chiles in it.

ORIENTAL STIR-FRY

Mix in a 1 cup measure
    ¼ CUP WATER
    2 TBS. SOY SAUCE
    ¼ TSP. SALT
Set aside.

Sauté for 10 minutes in a wok or a large heavy frying pan that can be covered
    1 LB. FIRM TOFU, CUT IN ½″ CUBES
    2-3 TSP. FINELY CHOPPED FRESH GINGER,* PEELED
    1 LARGE CLOVE GARLIC, MINCED OR PRESSED

In
    2-3 TBS. OIL
Stir often, scraping the bottom of the frying pan with a flat-edged spatula.

Add
    3-4 LARGE MUSHROOMS, THINLY SLICED
    ½ CUP (1 MEDIUM) CARROT, THINLY SLICED
    5-6 OZ. SNOW PEAS, STRUNG AND CUT IN HALF
Sauté a moment more, stirring constantly.

*Ginger is much easier to chop when it is frozen. Peel and wash the ginger root upon purchasing. Cut in appropriate sized pieces for your use and freeze. When a recipe calls for fresh ginger, remove the amount needed from the freezer and chop. Unused portions may be returned to the freezer.

Pour on
        THE RESERVED SAUCE
Cover and steam for 2-3 minutes.
Remove from heat.

Add
        8 OZ. MUNG OR SOY BEAN SPROUTS
Toss well.
Serve immediately.
Also makes a delicious cold luncheon entrée.
Serves 3-4.

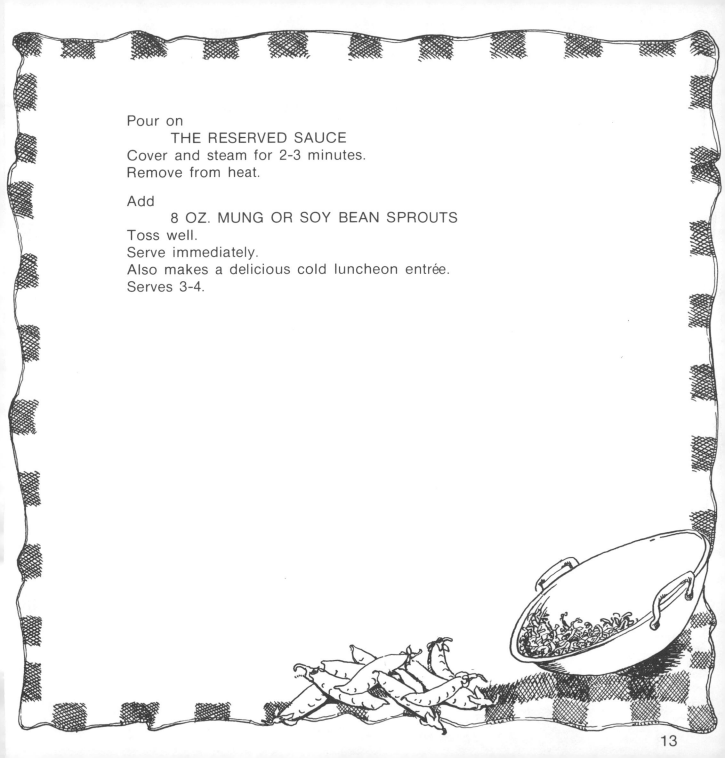

TOFU MEXICANO

Sauté in a large pot with a cover
    2 LARGE ONIONS, CHOPPED

In
    ¼ CUP OIL

Add and sauté a moment more
    1 TBS. + 2 TSP. MILD CHILI POWDER
    2 CLOVES GARLIC, MINCED OR PRESSED
    ½ LB. LARGE MUSHROOMS, SLICED (OPTIONAL)
Remove from heat.

Add
    2 LBS. ZUCCHINI, CUT IN THIN ROUNDS
    1 LB. CARROTS, CUT IN THIN ROUNDS
    1 LB. TOFU, MASHED WITH A POTATO MASHER
    2½ TSP. SALT
    1½ TSP. *EACH* CUMIN AND OREGANO

Cook, covered, for 20 minutes—until the veggies are just tender.
Stir occasionally.

Mound in pocket bread halves or taco shells, or pile on flat, crispy chapatis.*
Sprinkle with
    GRATED MONTEREY JACK CHEESE
Serves 6.

*See page 43.

CLEOPATRA'S EGGS

Sauté for about 5 minutes in a large oven-proof skillet with a cover
    1 ONION, CHOPPED
    STEMS FROM 1 BUNCH RED OR GREEN CHARD, CUT IN ½"
    PIECES
In
    2 TBS. BUTTER OR OIL
Add
    THE CHARD LEAVES, CHOPPED
    A FEW TABLESPOONS OF WATER
Cover and steam over medium-low heat for 3-5 minutes—until the leaves
are tender.
Remove from heat.

While the chard is steaming,
Mix in a medium-sized bowl
    4 EGGS
    1 CUP BUTTERMILK
    ½ CUP (1 OZ.) FRESHLY GRATED PARMESAN CHEESE
    ¼-½ TSP. SALT
    2 TSP. DRIED PARSLEY
    ⅛ TSP. BASIL
Pour over the steamed veggies.
Mix gently.
Bake at 350° for 25-30 minutes—until the center is firm.

Top with
    1-2 TOMATOES, SLICED IN ROUNDS
Cover the tomatoes with
    ½ CUP (1 OZ.) FRESHLY GRATED PARMESAN CHEESE

Broil to melt the cheese.
Serves 4.

OVEN FONDUE

Sauté in a 10" oven-proof skillet
  2 ONIONS, CHOPPED FINE

In
  2 TBS. OIL
Set aside.

Mix well in a medium-sized bowl
  1 LARGE TOMATO, DICED
  1¾ CUPS MILK
  4 EGGS
  ½ TSP. WORCESTERSHIRE SAUCE
  ¾ TSP. SALT

Add
  1 CUP (4 OZ.) GRATED MONTEREY JACK CHEESE
  2 CORN TORTILLAS, CUT IN ½" SQUARES
  THE SAUTÉED ONIONS
Mix again.

Pour back into the frying pan.
Bake at 350° for 30-40 minutes.
Let sit for 10 minutes before serving.
Serves 4.

OVEN OMELETTE

Sauté in a 9"-10" oven-proof skillet*
    ½ LB. MUSHROOMS, SLICED (OPTIONAL)
    1 CUP CHOPPED GREEN ONIONS

In
    2 TBS. BUTTER OR OIL

Remove from heat.

Mix in a medium-sized bowl
    1 CUP COTTAGE CHEESE
    5 EGGS
    1½ CUPS (6 OZ.) GRATED MONTEREY JACK CHEESE
    ¼ TSP. SALT (LESS IF MUSHROOMS ARE NOT USED)
    ½ TSP. BAKING POWDER

Add
    THE SAUTÉED VEGGIES
Mix well.

Return to the skillet.
Bake at 350° for 35-45 minutes—until the top begins to brown.

Serves 4.
Delicious with AVOCADO DRESSING (page 79).
See Spring Menu Suggestions (page 117).

*Instead of sautéing, try tossing the veggies in the oil and baking them in a 350°-400° oven for 8-10 minutes.

CRUSTLESS QUICHE

Sauté in a 10" oven-proof skillet with a cover
    1 LARGE ONION, CHOPPED FINE
    1 LARGE GARLIC CLOVE, MINCED OR PRESSED
    ½ LB. MUSHROOMS, THINLY SLICED

In
    3 TBS. BUTTER OR OIL
Remove from the pan.
Set aside.

Using the same pan, steam in a minimum amount of water until just tender
    10 OZ. SPINACH, CHOPPED
Set aside.

Mix together in a large bowl
    1 CUP MILK
    4 EGGS
    ½ TSP. OREGANO
    1-1½ TSP. SALT
    THE SAUTÉED VEGGIES
    2 CUPS (8 OZ.) GRATED JARLSBERG CHEESE

Add
    THE COOKED SPINACH, WELL DRAINED AND SLIGHTLY
      COOLED.
Stir gently to mix.

Pour back into the skillet.
Sprinkle with
        GRATED PARMESAN CHEESE (OPTIONAL)
Bake at 350° for 35 minutes, or until the center is firm.
Cool for 10 minutes before cutting.
Serves 6.

The best part of a quiche is usually the inside. Give a crustless quiche a try. It cuts down on preparation time and calories.

See Summer Menu Suggestions (page 118).

RED CHARD QUICHE

Sauté for about 5 minutes in a large oven-proof skillet with a cover
    1 ONION, CHOPPED
    THE STEMS FROM ONE BUNCH RED CHARD, CUT IN ½"
       PIECES
    ½ LB. MUSHROOMS, THINLY SLICED

In

    3 TBS. BUTTER OR OIL

Add

    THE CHARD LEAVES, CHOPPED
    A FEW TABLESPOONS OF WATER
Cover and steam over medium-low heat for 3-5 minutes—until the leaves
are tender.
Remove from heat.

While the chard is steaming,
Mix in a medium-sized bowl
    4 EGGS
    1½ CUPS MILK
    1 TBS. DRIED PARSLEY
    ½ TSP. SALT

Add
    2 CUPS (8 OZ.) GRATED JARLSBERG CHEESE
Mix well.
Pour over the steamed veggies.
Mix gently.
Bake at 350° for 35-40 minutes, or until the center is firm.
Serves 4.

ZUCCHINI PIZZA

THE ZUCCHINI

Mix in a large bowl
>2 LBS. GRATED ZUCCHINI
>2 TBS. FLOUR

Add
>2 EGGS, LIGHTLY BEATEN
>2 CUPS (8 OZ.) GRATED MONTEREY JACK CHEESE

Pat firmly into an oiled 10" x 15" jelly roll pan.
Bake at 400° for 25 minutes.
Remove from the oven.
Reduce the oven temperature to 350°.

THE SAUCE

Combine in a medium-sized saucepan
>1 CAN (15 OZ.) TOMATO SAUCE
>¼ TSP. *EACH* SALT AND GARLIC POWDER
>1 TSP. *EACH* OREGANO AND BASIL

Bring to a boil, reduce heat and simmer for 10 minutes.

ASSEMBLING THE PIZZA

Spread the tomato sauce evenly over the partially-baked zucchini.
Sprinkle with
>1½-2 CUPS (6-8 OZ.) GRATED MONTEREY JACK CHEESE

Bake at 350° for 20 minutes.
Let sit for 10 minutes before serving.
Serves 6-8.

HIGH PROTEIN ENCHILADAS

THE SAUCE

Combine in a medium-sized saucepan
> 1 CAN (15 OZ.) TOMATO SAUCE
> ½ CUP WATER
> 2½ TSP. CHILI POWDER
> ½ TSP. SALT
> ¼ TSP. CUMIN
> 2 CLOVES GARLIC, MINCED OR PRESSED (OR ½ TSP. GARLIC POWDER)

Bring to a boil, reduce heat and simmer for 10 minutes.

THE FILLING

Mix in a large bowl
> ½ CUP YOGURT
> 2 CUPS COTTAGE CHEESE
> 1 CUP FINELY CHOPPED GREEN ONION (ABOUT ONE BUNCH)
> 2 CUPS (8 OZ.) GRATED MONTEREY JACK CHEESE
> 1 CAN (4 OZ.) CHOPPED GREEN CHILES (OPTIONAL)

ASSEMBLING THE ENCHILADAS

12 CORN TORTILLAS

Pour about ½ cup of the tomato sauce into the bottom of a 9″ x 13″ pan.
Place a generous ¼ cup of the filling into the center of each tortilla.
Roll the tortilla around the filling.
Place seam-side down in the baking pan.
When all the tortillas have been filled, cover with
the remaining tomato sauce.

Top with
     1 CUP (4 OZ.) GRATED MONTEREY JACK CHEESE

Bake at 350° for 30-35 minutes.
Let stand for 10 minutes before serving.
Serves 6.
See Spring Menu Suggestions (page 116).

MEXICAN EGGPLANT

THE EGGPLANT

Cut into ½" rounds
>   1 EGGPLANT (ABOUT 1¼ LBS.)

Place on an oiled 12" x 15" baking pan with at least 1" sides.
Bake at 450° for 15-20 minutes.
Remove from the oven. Turn the oven down to 350°.

THE SAUCE

While the eggplant is baking,
Mix in a medium-sized bowl
>   1 CAN (15 OZ.) TOMATO SAUCE
>   ½ CUP (4 OZ.) CHILI SALSA
>   ½ CUP CHOPPED GREEN ONION
>   1 CLOVE GARLIC, MINCED OR PRESSED
>   ½ TSP. CUMIN

ASSEMBLING THE DISH

Pour the tomato sauce evenly over the partially baked eggplant.
Sprinkle with
>   2 CUPS (8 OZ.) GRATED MONTEREY JACK CHEESE

Bake at 350° for 25-30 minutes—till bubbly.

Serves 4.
Delicious with BAKED SQUASH (page 60).
See Winter Menu Suggestions (page 122).

ITALIAN EGGPLANT

THE EGGPLANT

Cut into ½" rounds
      1 EGGPLANT (ABOUT 1¼ LBS.)
Place on an oiled 12" x 15" baking pan with at least 1" sides.
Bake at 450° for 15-20 minutes.
Remove from the oven. Turn the oven down to 350°.

THE SAUCE

While the eggplant is baking,
Mix in a medium-sized bowl
      1 CAN (15 OZ.) TOMATO SAUCE
      1 CLOVE GARLIC, MINCED OR PRESSED
      ¼-½ CUP FINELY CHOPPED ONION
      ½ TSP. *EACH* BASIL, OREGANO AND THYME

ASSEMBLING THE DISH

Pour the tomato sauce evenly over the partially baked eggplant.
Sprinkle with
      1½ CUPS (6 OZ.) GRATED MONTEREY JACK CHEESE
      ½ CUP (2 OZ.) FRESHLY GRATED PARMESAN CHEESE

Bake at 350° for 25-30 minutes—till bubbly.
Serves 4.

POTATO CRUST QUICHE

THE CRUST

Steam over 1½"-2" of boiling water in a covered pan for 20-30 minutes—until tender

    4 WHITE POTATOES, THINLY PARED AND CUT IN QUARTERS

Transfer to a large mixing bowl and mash well.

Add

    1 EGG
    ½-¾ TSP. SALT
    ¼ TSP. NUTMEG

Mix well.

Press into a buttered 10" pan with 2" sides.
Prick the crust with a fork.
Bake at 425° for 12 minutes.
Remove from the oven.
Reduce the oven temperature to 325°.

THE FILLING

Sauté

    ½ LB. MUSHROOMS, SLICED

In

    2 TBS. BUTTER OR OIL

Add

    1 RED BELL PEPPER, CHOPPED (OPTIONAL)

Sauté until tender.

Set aside.

Mix well in a medium-sized bowl

    5 EGGS

    2 CUPS MILK

    1 TSP. SALT

    ½ TSP. NUTMEG

    1 CUP (4 OZ.) GRATED JARLSBERG CHEESE

ASSEMBLING THE QUICHE

Arrange the vegetables evenly over the bottom of the partially-baked crust.

Pour the egg mixture over the veggies.

Bake at 325° for 35-40 minutes, or until the filling is set.

Let stand for 15 minutes before serving.

Serves 4-6.

See Winter Menu Suggestions (page 122).

FIND-THE-TOFU LASAGNA

THE NOODLES

Cook according to package directions (salted water is not necessary)
    1 PACKAGE (12 OZ.) LASAGNA NOODLES
Rinse and set aside.

THE SAUCE

Sauté until clear in a large pot
    2 LARGE ONIONS, CHOPPED
    2 CLOVES GARLIC, MINCED OR PRESSED

In
    2-3 TBS. OIL

Add
    1 CAN (6 OZ.) TOMATO PASTE
    ¾ CUP (ONE TOMATO PASTE CAN FULL) WATER
    2 CANS (15 OZ. EACH) TOMATO SAUCE
    2 TSP. OREGANO
    1½ TSP. SALT
Simmer for 10 minutes.

THE FILLING

Combine in a large bowl
>   1 LB. FRESH TOFU, MASHED WITH A POTATO MASHER
>   1 LB. RICOTTA CHEESE
>   1 EGG
>   1 TSP. SALT
>   ¾ CUP (2 OZ.) FRESHLY GRATED PARMESAN CHEESE

Mix well.

Stir in
>   2 CUPS (8 OZ.) GRATED MONTEREY JACK CHEESE

ASSEMBLING THE LASAGNA

Spread ¼ of the simmered tomato sauce in the bottom of an oiled 9″x 13″ baking dish.
Cover evenly with ⅓ of the noodles (about 7), overlapping as necessary.
Spread ⅓ of the filling evenly over the noodles.

Repeat the layers twice.

Top with the remaining simmered sauce.
Sprinkle with
>   ½ CUP (2 OZ.) GRATED MONTEREY JACK CHEESE

Bake at 350° for 40-45 minutes—until bubbly.
Let stand for 10 minutes before cutting.
Serves 8-10.

SHABU-SHABU TERADA*

THE RICE

Bring to a boil in a heavy saucepan with a tight-fitting cover
    3 CUPS WATER
    ¼-½ TSP. SALT
Add slowly, stirring constantly
    1½ CUPS BROWN RICE
Bring back to a boil, reduce heat to low, cover and cook slowly until all the water is absorbed (about 50-60 minutes).

THE DIPPING SAUCES (Make early in the day so the flavors can blend.)

SESAME SAUCE

Mix in a small container with a lid
    2 TBS. TOASTED SESAME SEEDS
    2 TBS. SHIRO (WHITE) MISO
    1 TBS. RICE VINEGAR
    1 TBS. BROWN SUGAR
    ¼ TSP. CINNAMON
    A PINCH OF CLOVES
    ¼ CUP BROTH
Refrigerate to blend flavors.
Serve about 1 TBS. to each guest.

*Japanese Style Fondue

SOY-LEMON SAUCE

Mix in a small container with a lid
> 3 TBS. *EACH* SOY SAUCE AND LEMON JUICE
> 1 TSP. FRESH GINGER, GRATED*
> 1 TBS. BROWN SUGAR (OR MORE, TO TASTE)

Refrigerate to blend flavors.
Serve about 1 TBS. to each guest.

MILD MUSTARD SAUCE

Mix in a small container with a lid
> 3 TBS. MAYONNAISE
> 3 TBS. YOGURT
> 1½ TSP. DIJON MUSTARD
> 1 TBS. TAHINI

Refrigerate to blend flavors.
Serve about 1 TBS. to each guest.

THE DIPPERS

Arrange on one or more serving platters
> 3 CARROTS, SLICED IN ROUNDS AT A SLIGHT ANGLE
> 3 ZUCCHINI, SLICED IN ROUNDS
> 1 LARGE BUNCH FRESH SPINACH, STEMMED AND CUT IN 2"-3" PIECES
> 1 HEAD CHINESE CABBAGE, CUT IN 2"-3" PIECES
> ½-1 LB. LARGE MUSHROOMS, THICKLY SLICED
> 1 BUNCH GREEN ONIONS, TRIMMED AND CUT IN 1" LENGTHS
> 2 LBS. FIRM TOFU, CUT IN 1" CUBES

*Try grating ginger when it is frozen. See page 12.

Continued

THE BROTH

Warm in a shallow chafing dish (or an electric frying pan)
   1½ QUARTS (6 CUPS) BROTH

Serves 6.

TO SERVE

Set a plate, a rice bowl, chopsticks and three small saucers (for dips) at each place. (Alternatively, fondue plates with ridged sections may be used.)
Place the steaming broth in the center of the table over a gentle heat source.
Pass the dippers!

TO EAT

Choose a few dippers and place them in the broth to cook.
Retrieve a dipper that looks cooked just right. Dip it in a sauce and/or mix it with rice. Enjoy!
Adjust the temperature of the broth as necessary during the meal.

See Summer Menu Suggestions (page 118).

LEAPIN' LENTILS

Combine in a large pot with a cover
> 2 CUPS LENTILS, WASHED AND SORTED
> 5 CUPS WATER
> 1 TSP. SALT
> 2 BAY LEAVES
> A PINCH OF CLOVES
> 2½ TSP. POWDERED BOUILLON
> 2 TBS. APPLE CIDER VINEGAR
> 2 CLOVES GARLIC, MINCED OR PRESSED

Bring to a boil, reduce heat and simmer, covered, for 1½-2 hours—until the lentils are tender.
Stir occasionally.
Serves 4-6.

SERVING SUGGESTIONS

Good with rice and a green salad. Fun scooped into pocket bread and garnished with shredded lettuce, cherry tomatoes and avocado slices. Have a finger picnic! Serve lentils in a large bowl surrounded by red and/ or green bell pepper halves and good-sized leaves of tender lettuce. Fill the pepper halves and make lettuce roll-ups with LEAPIN' LENTILS. Offer deviled egg halves, tender corn-on-the-cob, and steamy french rolls to complete this finger-lickin' meal. (See Spring Menu Suggestions, page 116.)

LENTIL CHILI

Sauté in a large pot with a cover
      2 LARGE ONIONS, CHOPPED
      4 CLOVES GARLIC, MINCED OR PRESSED

In
      3 TBS. OIL OR BUTTER

Add and sauté for a moment more
      ¼ CUP MILD CHILI POWDER

Add
      9 CUPS WATER
      4⅔ CUPS LENTILS, WASHED AND SORTED
      2½ TSP. SALT

Bring to a boil, reduce heat and simmer, covered, until the lentils are tender—about 90 minutes.
Stir occasionally, adding water if necessary.*

Add
      2 CANS (15 OZ. EACH) TOMATO SAUCE
Mix well.
Simmer for 15-20 minutes, stirring often.

Serves 10-12.
Serve with rice, use in LENTIL BOWLADO (page 35) or in LENTIL DIP (page 83).

*LENTIL CHILI works very well as a make-ahead dish. Simmer lentils early in the day or even a few days ahead. Refrigerate—right in the cooking pan, if possible. Before serving, add the tomato sauce and simmer for 20-30 minutes.

LENTIL BOWLADO

Spoon *half* a recipe of hot LENTIL CHILI into a prewarmed bowl.

Serve with bowls of
     NATURAL TORTILLA CHIPS
     ⅓ HEAD ICEBERG LETTUCE, SHREDDED
     3 CARROTS, GRATED
     2 GREEN OR RED BELL PEPPERS, DICED
     ½ LARGE CUCUMBER, DICED
     2-3 LARGE TOMATOES, DICED
     2½-3 CUPS (10-12 OZ.) GRATED MONTEREY JACK CHEESE
     4 HARD-COOKED EGGS, CHOPPED
     2 LARGE AVOCADOS, DICED

Pass the lentils. Then pass the condiments and let everyone create his own LENTIL BOWLADO.

Serves 6.
See Summer Menu Suggestions (page 119).

PIZZA CRUST

Mix in a large bowl
>   2 TBS. BAKING YEAST
>   1½ CUPS WARM WATER (ABOUT 110°)

Stir to blend the yeast completely.

Add
>   ¾ TSP. *EACH* SALT, BASIL, OREGANO AND ONION POWDER
>   1 TBS. OLIVE OIL

Mix well.

Add 1 cup at a time, mixing well after each addition
>   4 CUPS UNBLEACHED FLOUR

When stirring becomes difficult, turn out onto a floured board and knead until smooth and somewhat glossy—about 5 minutes. Add more flour as needed (about ½ cup).

Place in a greased bowl; turn dough to grease top.
Cover and let rise in a warm place until doubled in bulk—about 1 hour. When doubled in bulk, punch down and divide in half with well-oiled hands. Pat out each half of the dough on a well-oiled 14″ pizza pan. Build up the edges a little to keep the sauce from spilling over.

Use with ITALIAN-STYLE VEGETARIAN PIZZA (page 37) and PIZZA OLÉ (page 38).

ITALIAN-STYLE VEGETARIAN PIZZA

THE CRUST

Make the pizza crust, page 36.

THE SAUCE

Sauté in a 2 quart pan
>   1 LARGE ONION, CHOPPED
>   1 CLOVE GARLIC, MINCED OR PRESSED

In
>   1-2 TBS. OIL

Add
>   1 CAN (15 OZ.) TOMATO SAUCE
>   ¼ TSP. SALT
>   ½ TSP. *EACH* OREGANO AND BASIL

Simmer for 10 minutes.

ASSEMBLING THE PIZZA

Top *each* crust with
>   HALF THE TOMATO SAUCE
>   ½ CUP (4 OZ.) CHOPPED BLACK OLIVES
>   ½ BUNCH GREEN ONIONS, CHOPPED
>   ½ LB. MUSHROOMS, SLICED (SAUTÉED IF DESIRED)
>   1-2 LARGE TOMATOES, CUT IN ¼" ROUNDS
>   1-2 LARGE GREEN OR RED BELL PEPPERS, CUT IN ¼" RINGS
>   1½-2 CUPS (6-8 OZ.) GRATED JACK OR MOZZARELLA CHEESE
>   ¼ CUP (1 OZ.) FINELY GRATED PARMESAN (OPTIONAL)

Bake at 450° for 20-25 minutes—until the crust begins to brown and the cheese is bubbly.
See Fall Menu Suggestions (page 121).

PIZZA OLÉ

THE CRUST

Make the pizza crust, page 36.

THE SAUCE

Sauté in a 2 quart pan
>   1 LARGE ONION, CHOPPED
>   2 CLOVES GARLIC, MINCED OR PRESSED

In
>   1-2 TBS. OIL

Add
>   1 CAN (15 OZ.) TOMATO SAUCE
>   1½ TSP. MILD CHILI POWDER
>   ¼-½ TSP. SALT
>   ½ TSP. *EACH* CUMIN AND OREGANO

Simmer for 10 minutes.

ASSEMBLING THE PIZZA

Spread evenly over *each* crust
>   2-3 CUPS REFRIED BEANS (PAGE40)
>   HALF THE TOMATO SAUCE

Top *each* crust with
>   4 OZ. DICED GREEN CHILES
>   ¼-⅓ CUP (2-3 OZ.) SLICED RIPE OLIVES
>   1½-2 CUPS (6-8 OZ.) GRATED JACK OR CHEDDAR CHEESE

Bake at 450° for 20-25 minutes—until the crust begins to brown and the cheese is bubbly.

LATIN BLACK BEANS

Combine in a large pot with a cover
> 3 CUPS BLACK BEANS, WASHED AND SORTED
> 12 CUPS WATER

Bring to a boil. Keep at a rolling boil for 15 seconds.
Remove from heat, cover, and let sit for one hour.

While the beans are soaking,
Sauté
> 3 ONIONS, CHOPPED FINE
> 3 CLOVES GARLIC, MINCED OR PRESSED

In
> 2-4 TBS. OIL

When the soaking time is up,
Add to the bean pot
> 3 BAY LEAVES
> 1 TBS. OREGANO
> ¼ CUP WINE VINEGAR (SCANT)
> 1 TBS. SALT
> ¼ TSP. TABASCO SAUCE
> THE SAUTÉED VEGETABLES
> 1 CAN (4 OZ.) CHOPPED GREEN CHILES

Bring to a boil, reduce heat and simmer, with the pot almost covered, for 3-3½ hours, or until the beans are tender.
Stir occasionally. Add water during cooking as necessary.

Serves 8-10.
Serve traditionally with rice and a green salad, or try with steamed cauliflower and DEVILED EGGS (page 84).
See page 125 for more information on cooking beans.

HOMEMADE REFRIED BEANS

Bring to a boil in a large pot with a cover
>   2½ CUPS PINTO BEANS, WASHED AND SORTED
>   1¼ TSP. SALT
>   7½ CUPS WATER

Simmer, with the pot almost covered, for 2½-3 hours—until the beans are soft enough to mash easily.
Stir occasionally, adding water as necessary to keep the beans covered.

Refrigerate at this point if you are cooking the beans ahead of time.*

About one-half hour before serving,
Sauté in a large skillet until clear
>   1 LARGE ONION, CHOPPED
>   1 CLOVE GARLIC, MINCED OR PRESSED

In
>   ½ CUP BUTTER

Add
>   ¾ TSP. CHILI POWDER
>   ⅜ TSP. CUMIN
>   1½ TSP. OREGANO
>   ½ TSP. SALT (OR TO TASTE)

Sauté a moment more.

Add
>   THE COOKED BEANS (SHOULD BE ABOUT 6 CUPS)

Mash the beans, over low heat, with a potato masher or a pastry blender.

*Either the beans alone or the recipe as a whole may be cooked 4 to 5 days ahead and refrigerated until needed.

Add
    ¾ CUP TOMATO SAUCE
Mix well. Heat through completely.
Serves 8.

Use in STACK-A-TORTILLA (see below), PIZZA OLÉ (page 38), CALI-
FORNIA PINTO PLATTER (page 44), homemade soups or ENCORE
DIPS (page 83).

See page 125 for more information on cooking beans.

STACK-A-TORTILLA

Spoon hot HOMEMADE REFRIED BEANS (page 40) into a prewarmed
bowl.

Serve with bowls of
    SHREDDED LETTUCE
    GRATED JACK OR CHEDDAR CHEESE
    TOMATO BITS
    GUACAMOLE*
    TACO SAUCE
    CRISP-FRIED OR OVEN-CRISPED** CORN TORTILLAS

At the table, STACK-A-TORTILLA! Start with a corn tortilla, add layers of
refried beans, cheese, lettuce, tomatoes and guacamole. Top with taco
sauce and dig in!

See Spring Menu Suggestions (page 117).

*See DON'S GUACAMOLE (page 82).
**Some brands of corn tortillas can be baked in a 350° oven for 8-10 minutes to a flaky crispness. If
  you want to avoid frying tortillas, look for fresh, thin, more delicate-looking tortillas and give the
  oven method a try.

REFRIED BLACK BEANS

Combine in a large pot with a cover
      2 CUPS BLACK BEANS, WASHED AND SORTED
      9 CUPS WATER
Bring to a boil. Keep at a rolling boil for 15 seconds.
Remove from heat, cover, and let sit for one hour.

Add
      1⅛ TSP. SALT
Simmer, with the pot almost covered, for 3 hours—until the beans are soft enough to mash easily.
Stir occasionally, adding water to keep the beans covered.

Refrigerate at this point if you are cooking the beans ahead of time.*

About one-half hour before serving,
Sauté in a large skillet until clear
      1 LARGE ONION, CHOPPED
      1 CLOVE GARLIC, MINCED OR PRESSED

In
      ½ CUP BUTTER

Add
      1 TBS.+ 1 TSP. MILD CHILI POWDER
      2 TSP. CUMIN
      1 TSP. CORIANDER
      ½ TSP. SALT (OR TO TASTE)
Sauté a moment more.

*Either the beans alone or the recipe as a whole may be cooked 4 to 5 days ahead and refrigerated until needed.

Add

THE COOKED BEANS (SHOULD BE ABOUT 6 CUPS)
Mash the beans over low heat, with a potato masher or a pastry blender.

Add a little water if necessary to reach desired consistency.
Mix well.
Heat through completely.
Serves 8.

Serve with rice, use in LATIN TOSTADAS (see below), ELLIOT'S BLACK BEAN EXTRAVAGANZA (page 45), or ENCORE DIPS (page 83).

See page 125 for more information on cooking beans.

LATIN TOSTADAS

LATIN TOSTADAS are first cousins of STACK-A-TORTILLAS (see page 41). They are just as much fun to make and equally challenging to eat.

Serve as suggested for STACK-A-TORTILLA, but substitute sour cream or yogurt for the guacamole. You may want to try chapatis* in place of corn tortillas as well. Experiment and enjoy!

*Chapatis are made from whole wheat flour and shaped very similarly to tortillas. They may be baked to crispness in 6-8 minutes in a 350° oven. Watch them closely, for they brown easily.

CALIFORNIA PINTO PLATTER

Cover a large platter (12"-13" in diameter) with a layer of
NATURAL CORN CHIPS, CRUSHED

Spoon on one recipe of
HOMEMADE REFRIED BEANS, WARMED THROUGH (PAGE 40)

Surround the beans with
½ CAN (6 OZ. DRAINED WEIGHT) WHOLE PITTED BLACK OLIVES

Sprinkle beans with
1-2 CUPS (4-8 OZ.) GRATED MONTEREY JACK CHEESE

Spoon on a recipe of
DON'S GUACAMOLE (PAGE 82)*

Layer with
⅓ MEDIUM-SIZED HEAD ICEBERG LETTUCE, SHREDDED
ALFALFA SPROUTS
½ BASKET CHERRY TOMATOES, QUARTERED
CHOPPED GREEN ONIONS

Top with
A DOLLOP OF SOUR CREAM OR YOGURT

Use a triangular shaped spatula for serving.
Serves 6-8.
See Summer Menu Suggestions (page 119).

*May be served separately, or, if you've invited several avocado lovers, make a double recipe—one for layering and one for extra garnishing.

ELLIOT'S BLACK BEAN EXTRAVAGANZA

Cover a large platter (12"-13" in diameter) with a layer of
     NATURAL CORN CHIPS, CRUSHED

Spoon on one recipe of
     REFRIED BLACK BEANS, WARMED THROUGH (page 42)

Sprinkle beans with
     1-2 CUPS (4-8 OZ.) GRATED MONTEREY JACK CHEESE

Spoon on a double recipe of
     EGG SALAD PIQUANT (page 85)

Layer with
     ⅓ MEDIUM-SIZED HEAD ICEBERG LETTUCE, SHREDDED
     ALFALFA SPROUTS
     ½ BASKET CHERRY TOMATOES, QUARTERED
     CHOPPED GREEN ONIONS

Drizzle with
     ½ CUP SOUR CREAM, mixed with
     ½ CUP GREEN CHILI SALSA

Use a triangular-shaped spatula for serving.
Serves 6-8.
See Summer Menu Suggestions (page 119).

JAN'S OVERNIGHT FALAFEL

Combine in a 6 cup container
    1 CUP DRIED GARBANZO BEANS
    4 CUPS WATER
Refrigerate overnight.

Chop to a medium-fine texture in a food processor*
    THE GARBANZO BEANS, THOROUGHLY DRAINED
    3 LARGE GREEN ONIONS, WASHED AND TRIMMED
    ½ CUP (PACKED) PARSLEY SPRIGS
    3 CLOVES GARLIC

Add and process just until blended (mixture should not be smooth)
    1 EGG
    1 TSP. *EACH* SALT AND CUMIN
Let stand for 30 minutes.

Form mixture into small balls—about 1" in diameter. (They will be fragile.)

*This recipe can also be made by grinding the first 4 ingredients in a food grinder and then hand mixing them with the rest of the ingredients.

Heat in a saucepan to 370°
      1¼″ OIL (OLIVE, TO BE AUTHENTIC)
Deep fry the falafel to a golden brown.
Drain on paper towels.

Makes about 24 falafel.
Serve as finger-lickin' hors d'oeuvres or in ARABIAN TACOS (page 48).

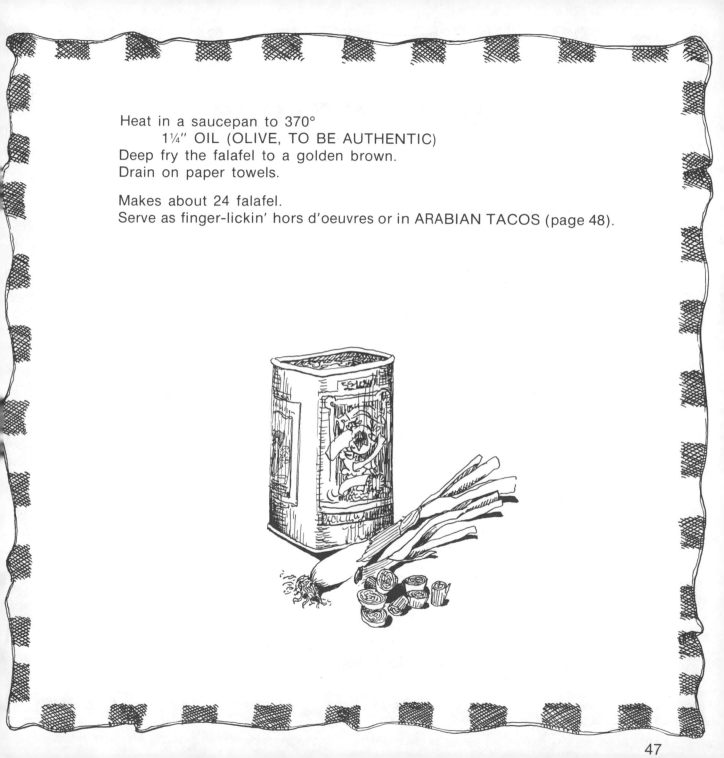

ARABIAN TACOS

Cut in half
   3 PITA (ALSO CALLED POCKET) BREADS

Fill each half with
   4 FALAFEL (PAGE 46)
   ¼ CUP SHREDDED LETTUCE OR BEAN SPROUTS
   4-6 CHERRY TOMATO QUARTERS
Top with either of the following sauces.

TAHINI-YOGURT SAUCE

Mix in a medium-sized bowl
   ⅓ CUP TAHINI
   ⅔ CUP YOGURT
   THE JUICE OF ONE LEMON
   A SPRINKLE OF GARLIC POWDER

TAHINI SAUCE

Mix in a medium-sized bowl
   ½-¾ CUP TAHINI
   ½ CUP WATER
   2 TBS. LEMON JUICE
   ½-1 TBS. SOY SAUCE

ARABIAN TACOS may be served with SIMPLY BROILED MUSHROOMS
(PAGE 52) and Ratatouille.*
See Winter Menu Suggestions (page 123).

*See page 123.

SURPRISE LOAF

Combine in a 6 cup container
   1 CUP DRIED SOY BEANS
   4 CUPS WATER
Refrigerate overnight.
Early the next day,
Mix thoroughly in a blender
   THE SOAKED SOY BEANS, THOROUGHLY DRAINED
   1 CUP TOMATO SAUCE
   1 CUP WATER
   ½ CUP PEANUT BUTTER
   1 TBS. BASIL
   2 TBS. OIL
   ¼ CUP SOY SAUCE
   2 EGGS

Stir in with a long-handled spoon
   1 CUP DRY OATMEAL

Pour into an oiled 4½" x 11½" bread pan.
Bake at 275° for about 3 hours, or until the center is firm.
Chill thoroughly before slicing.
Serve chilled or at room temperature.
Use as a main course or as a sandwich filling.

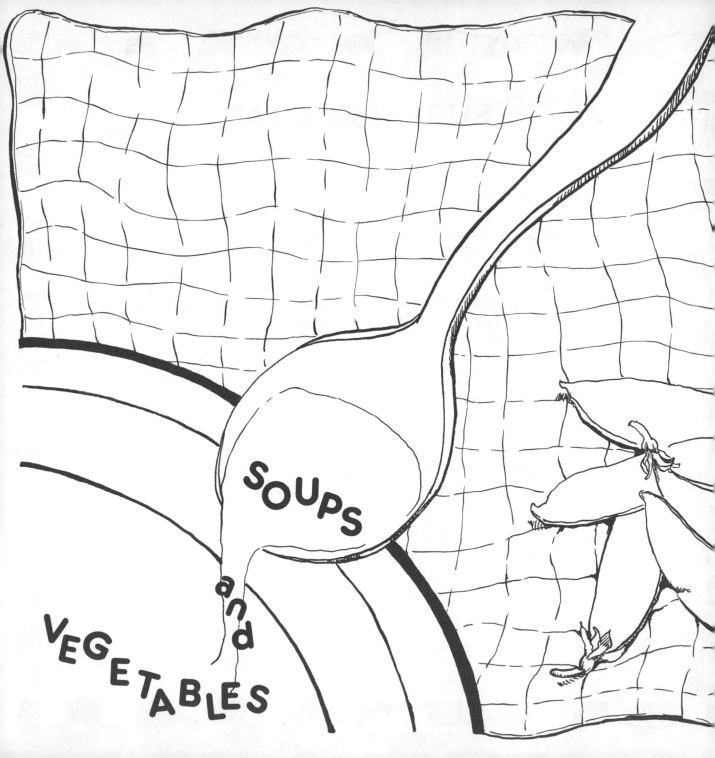

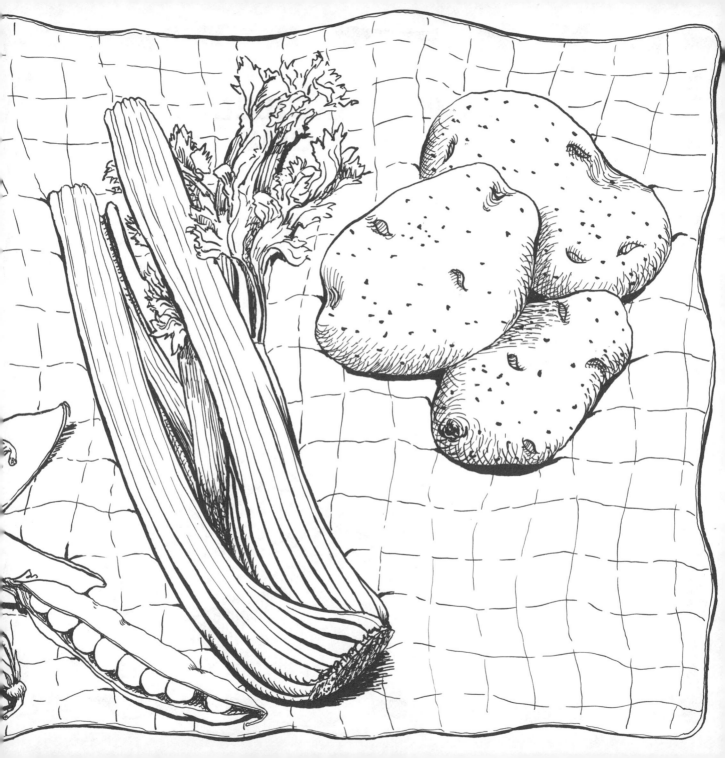

SIMPLY BROILED
MUSHROOMS

Clean and remove the stems from
    16 LARGE MUSHROOMS (NO GILLS SHOWING)
Place mushrooms, rounded sides down, in a shallow baking pan.

Put in each mushroom cavity
    ¼-½ TSP. BUTTER

Brush mushroom edges with
    MELTED BUTTER

Sprinkle lightly with
    LEMON JUICE
    SALT
    NUTMEG (OPTIONAL)

Broil for 5-8 minutes.
Serves 4-5.

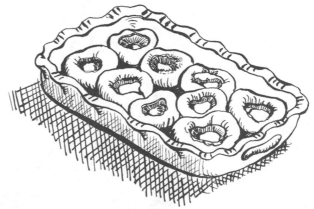

QUICK CHEESY ZUCCHINI

Steam over 1½"-2" of boiling water* in a covered pan until just tender
    3 LBS. ZUCCHINI, CUT IN ½" CUBES
Drain thoroughly.

Transfer *half* the zucchini to a warmed serving bowl.

Sprinkle with *half* of each of the following
    ½ TSP. OREGANO
    1 TSP. SALT (SCANT)
    1 CUP (4 OZ.) GRATED MONTEREY JACK CHEESE
Toss gently.

Top with the remaining zucchini.
Sprinkle with the remaining ingredients.
Toss again.

Serve immediately.
Serves 6.
Especially delicious with SURPRISE LOAF (page 49) and sliced tomatoes.

*Add ½ TSP. OREGANO to the water if you want additional oregano flavor.

HOT POTATOES!

Steam over 1½"-2" of boiling water in a covered pan for 15-20 minutes—until tender
>   3 LBS. WHITE POTATOES, SCRUBBED AND CUT IN ½" CUBES

While the potatoes are cooking,
Mix well in a large serving bowl
>   ¼ CUP YOGURT
>   ½ CUP MAYONNAISE
>   1 TBS. CORIANDER
>   2 TSP. OREGANO
>   1⅛ *EACH* CUMIN AND SALT

Add
>   1½ CUPS CHOPPED CELERY (½" PIECES)
>   THE COOKED POTATOES

Toss gently but thoroughly.

Garnish with (optional)
>   12 CHERRY TOMATOES, QUARTERED
>   ¼-½ CUP CHOPPED GREEN ONION

Serve immediately. Refrigerate encores* without delay.
Serves 6-8.

*See page 83. Try encores cold.

SWEET CURRIED CARROTS

Brown in large skillet with a cover
- 1½ TSP. TUMERIC
- ¾ TSP. DRY MUSTARD
- 1 TSP. CUMIN
- ½ TSP. CURRY POWDER
- ¼ TSP. *EACH* CLOVES AND CARDAMOM

In
- 1 TBS. BUTTER OR OIL

Add
- 1 CUP APPLE JUICE*
- ½ TSP. SALT
- 2 TBS. CURRANTS (OR RAISINS)

Stir and simmer briefly.

Add
1¾ LBS. LARGE CARROTS, CUT IN THIN ROUNDS
Bring to boil, reduce heat and simmer, covered, for 20-30 minutes—until the carrots are tender.
Serves 4-6.

*Or use ¼ cup frozen apple juice concentrate and ¾ cup water.

JILL'S VEGETABLES ITALIENNE

Sauté in a large frying pan with a cover

      6 ZUCCHINI, SLICED IN THIN ROUNDS
      4 CARROTS, SLICED IN THIN ROUNDS
      1 LARGE POTATO, CUBED
      1 ONION, CHOPPED

In

      ¼ CUP BUTTER OR OIL

Add

      10 OZ. FROZEN CORN
      10 OZ. FROZEN PEAS
      1 BOUILLON CUBE DISSOLVED IN ⅓ CUP WATER
      1 TSP. OREGANO
      1½ TSP. SALT

Bring to a boil, reduce heat and simmer, covered, for 45 minutes.*
Serves 4-6.

*In a hurry? Instead of simmering Jill's veggies for 45 minutes, pressure cook them for 2 minutes at 15 pounds pressure after sautéing them.

VEGETABLE MELANGE

Sauté in a 14" oven-proof skillet with a cover
    2 ONIONS, COARSELY CHOPPED
    1½ LBS. MUSHROOMS, COARSELY CHOPPED

In
    ¼ CUP OIL

Add
    2 LBS. ZUCCHINI, COARSELY CHOPPED
    ¾ LB. CARROTS, COARSELY GRATED
Sauté 2-3 minutes more, stirring.
Cover and simmer 8-10 minutes—until the veggies are tender crisp.

Remove from heat and sprinkle with
    1½ TSP. SALT
    ¼ CUP FLOUR
Mix well.

Add and mix thoroughly
    1½ CUPS MILK
    2½ CUPS (10 OZ.) FRESH OR FROZEN CORN
Bring to a boil, reduce heat and simmer for 2-3 minutes.

Add
    1½ CUPS (6 OZ.) GRATED MONTEREY JACK CHEESE
Mix thoroughly.

Clean off the edges of the pan.
Bake at 350° for 20 minutes—or until bubbly.
Serves 6-8.

CORNY ZUKE CASSEROLE

Sauté in a large oven-proof skillet
    1 ONION, CHOPPED

In
    2 TBS. BUTTER

Add
    1 LB. ZUCCHINI, GRATED
Sauté until clear.
Set aside.

Mix in a large bowl
    2 EGGS
    1½ CUPS (6 OZ.) GRATED MONTEREY JACK CHEESE
    ½ TSP. SALT
    2 OZ. CHOPPED GREEN CHILES
Add
    2½ CUPS (10 OZ.) FRESH OR FROZEN CORN
    THE SAUTÉED VEGGIES
Mix thoroughly.

Return to the skillet.
Bake at 350° for 35-45 minutes.

Serves 4.

POTATO CUSTARD

Mix well in a medium-sized bowl
    4 EGGS
    1 CUP MILK
    1¼ TSP. SALT
Pour into an oiled 9″ x 13″ baking dish.

Place *half* of each of the following, in layers, in the egg mixture
    1¾ LBS. POTATOES, SCRUBBED AND SLICED IN ⅜″ ROUNDS
    1 BUNCH GREEN ONIONS, CHOPPED
    2½ CUPS (10 OZ.) GRATED JARLSBERG OR OTHER FAVORITE
      CHEESE

Repeat the layers.

Bake at 350° for 45-50 minutes.
Serves 6-8.

BAKED SQUASH

Cut in half and remove the seeds and stringy part from
  2 ACORN SQUASH (OR USE 2-3 LBS. PRECUT BANANA
  SQUASH)

Place cut side up, in a baking dish.
Pour water into the dish to cover the bottom ⅛″-¼″ deep.
Cover the baking dish with foil.
Bake at 400° for 30 minutes.

Reduce the oven temperature to 350° and bake until the squash feels tender when pierced with a fork.
Serves 4.

APPLE-STUFFED SQUASH

Mix in a medium-sized bowl
  2 MEDIUM BAKING APPLES, GRATED
  2 TBS. RAISINS
  2 TBS. MAPLE SYRUP
  ½ TSP. CINNAMON
  2 TBS. CHOPPED WALNUTS

Set aside.

Prepare the squash for baking as suggested above.
After placing the squash in the baking dish, spoon an equal amount of stuffing into the center of each squash piece.
Cover and bake as suggested above.

This filling can also be used as a dessert. Bake separately and serve warm with milk or cream, or stir chilled, unbaked filling into yogurt.

GAZPACHO

Blend in a 5-6 cup glass container with a lid
      1 LARGE TOMATO, CHOPPED
      ½ LARGE GREEN PEPPER, CHOPPED
      2 MEDIUM CELERY RIBS, CHOPPED
      ½ CUP CHOPPED CUCUMBER
      2 LARGE CHOPPED GREEN ONIONS
      2 TSP. SNIPPED PARSLEY (OR ½ TSP. DRIED PARSLEY)
      ½ TSP. GARLIC POWDER
      2 TBS. WHITE WINE VINEGAR
      ½ TBS. WORCESTERSHIRE SAUCE
      2 CUPS TOMATO JUICE
      SALT TO TASTE (ABOUT ¼ TSP.)

Chill overnight.
Serves 6.

CORN CHOWDER

Sauté until clear in a medium-large pot
      1 LARGE ONION, CHOPPED FINE

In
      3 TBS. OIL

Add
      2 LARGE POTATOES, SCRUBBED AND CUT IN ¼" CUBES
Sauté a few moments longer.

Add
      4 CUPS MILK
      2 TSP. SALT
      ¼ TSP. PAPRIKA
      2½ CUPS (10 OZ.) FRESH OR FROZEN CORN

Bring to a boil, reduce heat and simmer for 15-20 minutes.
Stir occasionally.
Serves 4.

ZESTY SOY SOUP

Sauté in a medium-large pot with a cover
     1 LARGE ONION, CHOPPED FINE
     1 CLOVE GARLIC, MINCED OR PRESSED

In
     2 TBS. BUTTER OR OIL

Add
     2 CUPS COOKED SOY BEANS
     2 CUPS WATER
     1 CAN (15 OZ.) TOMATO SAUCE
     ½ TSP. SALT (LESS IF THE BEANS ARE SALTED)
     2-4 TBS. CHOPPED GREEN CHILES
Bring to a boil, reduce heat and simmer, covered, for 10 minutes.
Add
     2½ CUPS (10 OZ.) FRESH OR FROZEN CORN
     2 CORN TORTILLAS, CUT IN ½" SQUARES
Return to a boil, reduce heat and simmer, covered, for an additional 5 minutes.
Garnish each serving with
     ¼ CUP (1 OZ.) GRATED MONTEREY JACK CHEESE
     DICED AVOCADO
     ADDITIONAL CHOPPED GREEN CHILES

Serves 4-6.

GLORIA'S LENTIL VEGETABLE SOUP

Combine in a large soup pot with a cover
      2 CUPS LENTILS, WASHED AND SORTED
      8 CUPS WATER
      1 ONION, COARSELY CHOPPED
      1 CLOVE GARLIC, MINCED OR PRESSED
      2 LARGE CARROTS, CUT IN THICK ROUNDS
      2 LARGE CELERY RIBS, CUT IN ½" PIECES
      1 ZUCCHINI, CUT IN ½" HALF-ROUNDS
      2 LARGE POTATOES, CUT IN ½" CUBES
      1 TBS. DRIED PARSLEY
      ½ TSP. OREGANO
      2½ TSP. SALT
Bring to a boil, reduce heat and simmer, covered, for 1½ hours.

Add
      1 CAN (28 OZ.) TOMATOES
      2 TBS. WINE VINEGAR
      10-12 OZ. FROZEN PEAS
Return to a boil, reduce heat and simmer, covered, for an additional 30 minutes.
Serves 6-8.

See Winter Menu Suggestions (page 123).

SPLIT PEA SOUP

Sauté in a large soup pot with a cover
>2 LARGE CELERY RIBS, CHOPPED
>2 LARGE CARROTS, CHOPPED
>1 LARGE ONION, CHOPPED

In
>¼ CUP OIL OR BUTTER

Add
>3 QUARTS WATER
>3¼ CUPS SPLIT PEAS
>2 TSP. SALT
>1½ TSP. WORCESTERSHIRE SAUCE
>3 TBS. SOY SAUCE
>2 LARGE BAY LEAVES

Bring to a boil, reduce heat and simmer, covered, for 2-2½ hours.
Stir occasionally, especially during the last hour.

Stir well before serving.
Serves 8-10.
See Winter Menu Suggestions (page 122).

THANKSGIVING PUMPKIN SOUP

Halloween's pumpkin farms hold more than future jack-o'-lanterns. Find a Thanksgiving centerpiece there, too. Choose a squatty pumpkin that will be able to wait patiently in a cool, dry place in your garage. On Thanksgiving day, fill your spruced-up pumpkin with a warm, tasty soup.

THE SQUASH

Two or three days before Thanksgiving, plan a dinner featuring baked banana squash (see page 60). Prepare enough squash to reserve about 6 cups of cubed squash. Refrigerate, covered or wrapped.

THE PUMPKIN

Cut a 6" circle around the stem of a
    10" DIAMETER PUMPKIN, WELL SCRUBBED
Remove the seeds and the stringy part from the inside.

For the 15 minutes just before serving, bake on an ovenproof platter at 350°.

THE EXTRAS

Prepare the following. Place each in a separate serving bowl
>4 CUPS (1 LB.) GRATED MONTEREY JACK CHEESE
>4 CUPS TOASTED PUMPKIN SEEDS
>4 LARGE AVOCADOS, CUBED
>6-8 CUPS COOKED BROWN RICE (TO BE SERVED HOT)*

THE SOUP

Sauté in a large pot
>2 LARGE ONIONS, CHOPPED FINE
>2 CLOVES GARLIC, MINCED OR PRESSED

In
>2-3 TBS. OIL

Add
>3 QUARTS (12 CUPS) SEASONED VEGETABLE BROTH OR CHICKEN BROTH

Bring to a boil and add
>20 OZ. FROZEN CORN
>6 CUPS CUBED, PRECOOKED BANANA SQUASH

Heat through.

Pour into the prewarmed pumpkin and set on a sturdy trivet in the center of your Thanksgiving table.

Serve the soup from the pumpkin.
Pass the bowls of "extras" and allow each person to create his own unique Thanksgiving treat.
Serves 8.
See Fall Menu Suggestions (page 121).

*See page 30.

Want to perk up interest in salads? Set the table with icy forks and chilly salad plates retrieved from the freezer at just the right moment—or offer a great selection of goodies and encourage each person to make his own unique concoction right at the table.

SALADS DRESSINGS DIPS & SPREADS

SUMMER FRUIT SALAD

Combine in a serving bowl
      1 BASKET (12-14 OZ.) STRAWBERRIES, HULLED AND CUT IN HALF
      3-4 VERY RIPE FREESTONE PEACHES, CUT IN BITE-SIZED PIECES
      2 CUPS THOMPSON SEEDLESS GRAPES
      1-2 RIPE BANANAS, CUT IN ROUNDS
      1 RIPE PINEAPPLE, CORED AND CUBED (OR 1 CAN (20 OZ.) JUICE-PACKED PINEAPPLE CHUNKS, WELL DRAINED)

Serves 6-8.
For a crowd triple the recipe and serve in a punch bowl.

SPICY ISLANDS FRUIT SALAD

Mix in a large salad bowl
     3 TBS. LEMON JUICE
     ¾ TSP. CURRY POWDER
     1 TBS. VERY MILD HONEY

Add
     1 CAN (20 OZ.) JUICE-PACKED PINEAPPLE CHUNKS
     2 LARGE SEEDED ORANGES, SECTIONED AND CUT IN
       THIRDS
     2-4 BANANAS, CUT IN ROUNDS
     1-2 AVOCADOS, CUT IN ½" CUBES (OPTIONAL)
     ½-1 CUP COARSELY CHOPPED MACADAMIA NUTS*

Toss gently.
Refrigerate for at least one hour to let flavors blend.

Serves 4-6.

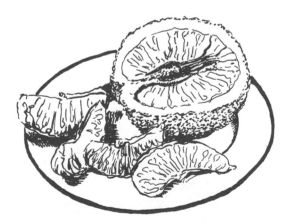

* Toasted almonds can be substituted.

CHEPLE DATE SALAD

Combine in a large bowl
      2 LARGE TASTY APPLES, DICED
      1 TBS. LEMON JUICE OR VINEGAR
Toss well.

Add
      2 LARGE CELERY RIBS, DICED
      ⅓ CUP CHOPPED DATES (ABOUT 8 LARGE)
      1½ CUPS (6 OZ.) JARLSBERG CHEESE, CUT IN ¼″ CUBES
      ¼ TSP. SALT
      ⅛ TSP. CUMIN
      1 TBS. OIL

Toss again.
Refrigerate to blend flavors.

Serves 4-6.

COTTAGE CARROT SALAD

Mix in a large bowl
      1 CUP COTTAGE CHEESE
      ¼ CUP MAYONNAISE
      ⅓ CUP YOGURT
      1 CUP CURRANTS*
      ½ TSP. LEMON PEEL

Add
      6 MEDIUM CARROTS, GRATED
Toss well.

Nice served with a sprinkle of chopped walnuts.
Serves 4-6.

*Raisins may be substituted, but they take longer to release their sweetness.

SWEET SPINACH SALAD

Combine in a small jar with a tight-fitting lid
    2 TBS. WHITE WINE VINEGAR
    6 TBS. OIL
    2 TSP. MILD HONEY
    ¼ TSP. *EACH* SALT, CURRY POWDER AND DRY MUSTARD
    A BIT OF FINELY CHOPPED ONION (OR ¼ TSP. ONION
    POWDER)
    1 TBS. TOASTED SESAME SEEDS*
Let sit for several hours at room temperature, or refrigerate overnight to allow flavors to blend.

Combine in a large salad bowl
    1½ LBS. FRESH SPINACH, WASHED, CRISPED AND TORN
       INTO BITE-SIZED PIECES
    2 TASTY APPLES, DICED OR COARSELY GRATED
    ½ CUP ROASTED SPANISH PEANUTS (OPTIONAL)
    ⅓ CUP RAISINS
    THE DRESSING
Serve at once.
Serves 6-8.

*To toast sesame seeds sprinkle into a dry frying pan. Place over low heat until slightly browned. Stir often.

LIZ'S FRESH MUSHROOM SALAD

Combine in a large serving bowl
    ½ LB. OF THE FRESHEST MUSHROOMS YOU CAN FIND (NO
       GILLS SHOWING), THINLY SLICED
    2 TBS. FRESH LEMON JUICE
Toss lightly, but thoroughly.

Add
    ¼ CUP FINELY CHOPPED GREEN ONION
    ¼ TSP. SALT
    1 TBS. OIL

Toss again.
Chill for approximately 1 hour.
Serves 3.

SALAD SPECTACULAR

Arrange on one or two large platters several of the following
> WASHED, DRIED, AND CHILLED SALAD GREENS
> SMALL FLOWERETS OF CAULIFLOWER AND BROCCOLI
> ROUNDS OF CUCUMBER, ZUCCHINI, CROOKED NECK
>   SQUASH
> DICED CELERY AND CARROTS
> SPROUTS
> CHERRY TOMATOES
> JICAMA CUBES, SNOW PEAS, ASPARAGUS TIPS (IN SEASON)
> MUSHROOM SLICES
> GREEN ONION SLIVERS
> GREEN OR RED BELL PEPPER BITS

Put several of the following in small bowls
> CHOPPED NUTS
> TOASTED SESAME OR SUNFLOWER SEEDS
> FETA CHEESE OR BLEU CHEESE CRUMBLES
> GRATED CHEESE
> CHOPPED HARD-COOKED EGG BITS
> AVOCADO CUBES
> WATER CHESTNUT SLIVERS
> PICKLE BITS

Pour into pitchers (or bowls with small ladles)

2-3 SALAD DRESSINGS

Serve buffet style, or pass the veggie platter(s), bowls and dressings and let everyone create his own SALAD SPECTACULAR.

Encores* from a SALAD SPECTACULAR can be used in next evening's soup or salad, in lunchtime veggie and cottage cheese stirs, in sandwiches, or as toppers for tostadas.
See Summer Menu Suggestions (page 119).

*See page 83.

BRENT'S BLEU CHEESE DRESSING

Mix in a medium-sized bowl
   ½ CUP MAYONNAISE (SCANT)
   ½ CUP YOGURT
   ¼ CUP WINE VINEGAR
   1 TSP. PREPARED MUSTARD
   3 TBS. MILK
   ⅛ TSP. SALT

Add
   ½ LB. BLEU CHEESE, CRUMBLED

Mix gently.
Refrigerate for several hours before serving to let flavors blend.

COLORFUL AVOCADO DRESSING

Mash in a medium-sized bowl
    1 RIPE AVOCADO

Add

    2 TBS. LEMON JUICE
    ¼ TSP. TABASCO SAUCE
    ¼–½ TSP. SALT
    ⅛ TSP. WORCESTERSHIRE SAUCE
    ¾ CUP BUTTERMILK
    1 FINELY CHOPPED GREEN ONION

Mix well.

Add

    2 TBS. SUNFLOWER SEEDS
    10-12 CHERRY TOMATOES, QUARTERED

Mix gently.
Pour over shredded lettuce nestled in a curly lettuce leaf.

KEEP IT SIMPLE EVERYDAY SALAD DRESSINGS

SALSA'D THOUSAND ISLAND DRESSING

Mix in a small container with a lid
      6 TBS. MAYONNAISE (OR 4 TBS. MAYO AND 2 TBS. YOGURT)
      3 TBS. GREEN CHILI SALSA
Refrigerate until needed.

CURRIED DRESSING

Mix in a small container with a lid
      3 TBS. *EACH* MAYONNAISE AND YOGURT
      ¾ TSP. *EACH* LEMON JUICE AND MILD FLAVORED HONEY
      ⅜ TSP. *EACH* CURRY POWDER, ONION POWDER AND
         GARLIC POWDER
Refrigerate until needed.

DIJON-PLUS DRESSING

Mix in a small container with a lid
      3 TBS. *EACH* MAYONNAISE AND YOGURT
      1½ TSP. DIJON MUSTARD
Refrigerate until needed.

Join the Mayo-Yogurt Conspiracy.

Mayonnaise   100 calories per tablespoon
Yogurt   9-10 calories per tablespoon

Try lowering the mayonnaise calories in your own favorite recipes by substituting yogurt for some of the mayonnaise. Start by using ¼ yogurt and ¾ mayo. Increase the yogurt proportion over time.

ALL SEASONS SALAD SEASONING

Mix together in a jar with a tight-fitting cover
> 1 TSP. SALT
> ½ TSP. PAPRIKA
> ¼ TSP. DILL WEED
> ⅛ TSP. GARLIC POWDER
> ¼ TSP. ONION POWDER
> 1 TBS. DRIED PARSLEY
> 1 CUP VERY FINELY GRATED PARMESAN CHEESE

Store, tightly covered, in a cool place.

Sprinkle on oil and vinegar dressed salads, or mix with your favorite creamy dressing base.

Also good on baked potatoes, other cooked veggies, and in dips and sauces.

In a small decorative bottle, ALL SEASONS SALAD SEASONING becomes a thoughtful holiday gift.

DON'S GUACAMOLE

Mash with a fork in a medium-sized bowl
    4 RIPE AVOCADOS

Add
        ½ CUP GREEN CHILI SALSA
        1 TBS. + 1 TSP. LEMON JUICE
        ¼ TSP. SALT
        ⅛ TSP. GARLIC POWDER (USE FRESH GARLIC IF YOU LIKE A
            SHARPER GARLIC FLAVOR)
        ¼ CUP SOUR CREAM (OPTIONAL)
        A FEW DROPS OF TABASCO SAUCE (OPTIONAL)

Mix until fairly smooth.

ENCORE DIPS

LENTIL CHILI, LEAPIN' LENTILS, REFRIED BLACK BEANS and HOMEMADE REFRIED BEANS make delicious dips when they have been thoroughly chilled and mixed to taste with mayonnaise and extra salt.

Serve as a dip with natural corn chips or veggie chips, use as a sandwich filling or layer in a thermos with cottage cheese for an away-from-home lunch.

What's an ENCORE ?
An ENCORE is a second chance to enjoy a tasty dish without having to prepare it—just dish it up, mix it up or layer it. ENCORE—a much more appealing label than leftover!

DEVILED EGGS

Place in a saucepan with a cover
      6 EGGS

Add
      WATER TO COVER THE EGGS BY 1″
Cover and bring quickly to a boil.
Reduce heat to very low.
Cook the eggs for 15 minutes.

Drain the water from the pan.
Top the eggs with ice cubes and fill the pan with cold water.
(Chilling the eggs quickly will help eliminate the dark ring that forms around yolks when eggs are cooked too long.)
Peel the eggs and cut them in half lengthwise with a sharp, thin knife.
Gently remove the yolks.

Mix in a medium-sized bowl
      THE EGG YOLKS, CRUMBLED WITH A FORK
      2 TBS. MAYONNAISE
      2 TBS. YOGURT
      ¼ TSP. PREPARED MUSTARD (OR DIJON MUSTARD)
      ⅛ TSP. SALT
      ¼ TSP. *EACH* CURRY POWDER AND ONION POWDER

Mound the yolk mixture into the egg white hollows.
Refrigerate until served.

CHEESY DEVILED EGGS

Add to the basic deviled egg recipe
⅓ CUP FINELY GRATED CHEESE

NUTTY EGGS

Add to the basic deviled egg recipe
¼ CUP CHOPPED WALNUTS OR ALMONDS

EGG SALAD PIQUANT

Combine in a medium-sized bowl
6 HARD- COOKED EGGS, PEELED AND CHOPPED
3 TBS. MAYONNAISE
1 TBS. YOGURT
¼ TSP. POWDERED MUSTARD
1 TBS. CHOPPED GREEN CHILES
⅛ TSP. SALT (OR TO TASTE)

Add (Optional)
A FEW DASHES OF TABASCO SAUCE
SOME CHOPPED GREEN ONIONS

Serve as an appetizer on a bed of lettuce accompanied by a basket of
tortilla (corn) chips, in lunchtime sandwiches, on morning toast, or in
ELLIOT'S BLACK BEAN EXTRAVAGANZA (page 45).

SWEET PEANUT BUTTER SPREAD

Mix well in a small container with a lid
     ½ CUP PEANUT BUTTER
     2 TBS. MILD HONEY
     ½ TSP. CINNAMON

Add
     ¼ CUP APPLE JUICE CONCENTRATE
Stir to blend completely.

Add
     ¼ CUP CURRANTS (OR CHOPPED RAISINS)
Stir again.

Spread on bread, toast, apple quarters and banana rounds.

CRUNCHY CREAM CHEESE SPREAD

Combine in a medium-sized container with a tight-fitting lid
    ½ CUP CREAM CHEESE, AT ROOM TEMPERATURE
    ¼ CUP COARSELY CRUSHED DRIED BANANA CHIPS
    2 TBS. CURRANTS
    2 TBS. CHOPPED WALNUTS
    HONEY TO TASTE (TRY 1 TBS. FOR STARTERS)
Mix well with a fork.

Great on raisin bread, brown bread or stuffed in large pitted dates.

SWEET
TREATS

POLYNESIAN SMOOTHY

Mix in a blender until smooth
    1 LARGE, VERY RIPE BANANA
    2 CUPS JUICE-PACKED CRUSHED PINEAPPLE
    2 CUPS ORANGE JUICE (OR ½ CUP FROZEN ORANGE JUICE
       CONCENTRATE AND 1½ CUPS WATER)
    1 CUP MILK
    1 TBS. MILD HONEY
    2 TSP. LEMON JUICE
    1 TSP. VANILLA

Add
    1 TRAY ICE CUBES (ABOUT   SIXTEEN LARGE CUBES)

Blend to a slush.
Serve immediately.
Serves 6-8.

ELEGANT WINTER FRUIT DESSERT

Combine in a small saucepan
> THE JUICE FROM A 20 OZ. CAN OF JUICE-PACKED CRUSHED
> PINEAPPLE
> 1 TSP. ARROWROOT

Bring to a boil, reduce heat and simmer to thicken.

Add
> THE DRAINED PINEAPPLE

Chill.

Mix in a large serving bowl
> 5 ORANGES, SECTIONED AND CUT IN HALF
> 2 BANANAS, CUT IN ROUNDS
> 2 SOFT-RIPE HACHIYA PERSIMMONS,* PEELED AND CUT IN
> SMALL PIECES
> THE CHILLED PINEAPPLE

TO SERVE

Pass the fruit bowl.
Then, as garnishes, pass bowls of
> SHREDDED COCONUT
> SHELLED PISTACHIOS
> CREAMY DRESSING (PAGE 92)

*See page 112.

LEMONY STEWED FRUIT

Combine in a 1½ quart saucepan with a cover
>   12 DRIED FIGS OR APPLE RINGS, CUT IN 2 OR 3 PIECES
>   12 PRUNES
>   24 DRIED APRICOT HALVES
>   ⅓ CUP RAISINS
>   ½ TSP. LEMON PEEL
>   3 CUPS WATER

Bring to a boil, reduce heat and simmer, covered, for about 15 minutes—until the fruit is tender. Stir once or twice while simmering. Add water if necessary.

Try chilled LEMONY STEWED FRUIT with CREAMY DRESSING.

CREAMY DRESSING

Combine in a container with a lid
>   1 CUP YOGURT
>   1 CUP SOUR CREAM
>   2 TBS. MILD HONEY
>   1 TSP. VANILLA
>   A PINCH OF SALT

Refrigerate until served.

Serves 6-8.

HEAVENLY CREME

Soften

    1 TBS. UNFLAVORED GELATIN

In

    2 TBS. WATER

Heat to dissolve completely.
Set aside.

Blend in a blender until smooth
    3 PEACHES OR NECTARINES, WASHED AND QUARTERED
    1 CUP YOGURT
    3-4 TBS. BROWN SUGAR
    A FEW DROPS OF ALMOND EXTRACT

Add

    THE GELATIN MIXTURE
Blend again.
Pour into a serving bowl.
Chill until set.
Serves 3-4.

APPLE DELIGHT

Mix in a large bowl
>   3 LARGE COOKING APPLES, WASHED, CORED AND THINLY
>   SLICED
>   1 TBS. + 1 TSP. LEMON JUICE
>   ½ TSP. CINNAMON

Spoon into an ungreased 9" casserole.

Combine in a medium-sized bowl
>   ½ CUP DRY OATMEAL
>   3 TBS. INSTANT NONFAT MILK POWDER
>   2 TBS. WHOLE WHEAT PASTRY FLOUR*
>   ¼ CUP BROWN SUGAR
>   ½ TSP. CINNAMON
>   ⅛ TSP. SALT

Add and cut in with a pastry blender till crumbly
>   3-4 TBS. BUTTER, SOFTENED

Spread the oat mixture over the apples.
Bake at 350° for 30 minutes.

Serve warm—with cream or ice cream if desired.
Serves 3-4.

*See page 124.

BAKED APPLES

Wash and core
      6 BAKING APPLES

Fill each cavity with a mixture of
      RAISINS
      DATES
      CHOPPED WALNUTS
Place in a baking dish.

Pour about ¼" of water in the baking dish.
Cover loosely with foil.

Bake at 350° for 30-50 minutes—until the apples are tender
when pierced with a fork.

YOGURT CREAM PIE

THE CRUST

Prepare your favorite crumb crust.
Bake if necessary.
Chill until needed.

THE FILLING

Soften
> 1 TBS. UNFLAVORED GELATIN

In
> ½ CUP WATER

Heat to dissolve completely.

Mix in a blender until smooth
> 4 OZ. CREAM CHEESE
> 1 CUP YOGURT
> ⅜ CUP VERY MILD HONEY OR OTHER SWEETENER
> 2 TSP. VANILLA
> 1 TSP. (PACKED) LEMON PEEL*
> THE GELATIN MIXTURE

Chill until the mixture is slightly thickened.

*See page 124.

Whip until stiff

    ¾ CUP WHIPPING CREAM*

Fold the gelatin mixture gently into the whipped cream.

Turn into the prepared crust.
Chill until set.

YOGURT DATE CREAM PIE

Make a delicious YOGURT DATE CREAM PIE by folding chopped dates into the gelatin mixture just before adding it to the whipped cream.

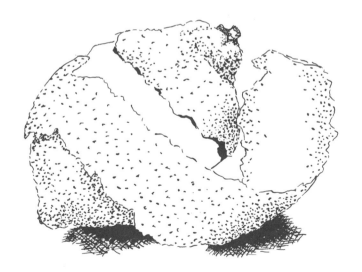

*Extra whipped cream? See page 124.

PUMPKIN PUDDING

Combine in a large mixing bowl
> 6 EGGS
> 1 CUP BROWN SUGAR
> ⅓ CUP UNSULPHURED SWEET MOLASSES (GRAMMA'S IS ONE NAME BRAND)
> 2 TSP. CINNAMON
> 1 TSP. *EACH* SALT AND GINGER
> ½ TSP. *EACH* NUTMEG, CLOVES AND ALLSPICE

Mix well.

Add
> 1 CUP INSTANT NONFAT MILK POWDER
> 3 CUPS WHOLE MILK
> 1 CAN (29 OZ.) PUMPKIN

Mix thoroughly.

Pour into a 9" x 13" baking pan.
Bake at 325° for 50-60 minutes—until the center is quite firm.

Cool completely.
Keep refrigerated.

MAKE-YOUR-OWN SUNDAES

Offer bowls of complementary sauces, sprinkles and/or toppers for your favorite ice cream. Let everyone create his own ice cream dream.

SAUCE IDEAS

SLICED RIPE FREESTONE PEACHES, SLIGHTLY CRUSHED TO RELEASE JUICES

CRUSHED FRESH STRAWBERRIES, BLACKBERRIES, OR BOYSENBERRIES

CRUSHED PINEAPPLE, CANNED IN ITS OWN JUICE

RICH CHOCOLATE OR CAROB SAUCE—Bring a mixture of chips and water to a boil over low heat. Stir vigorously to make satiny...Experiment to find just the right thickness for you. (The sauce thickens as it cools.)

SPRINKLES POSSIBILITIES

SHREDDED COCONUT

CHOPPED WALNUTS, TOASTED ALMONDS, PISTACHIOS, OR MACADAMIA NUTS

GRANOLA

SPANISH PEANUTS

ALL-TIME TOP TOPPER

FRESH CREAM WITH A TOUCH OF VANILLA WHIPPED TO PEAKS*

*Extra whipped cream? See page 124.

BAKED ALASKA

Place on a freezer-to-oven serving platter*
>A 7" x 9" PIECE OF YOUR FAVORITE CAKE (OR AN OVERSIZED
>HOME BAKED COOKIE)

Top with
>½ GALLON BRICK-PACKED NATURAL ICE CREAM

Freeze while you prepare the meringue.

THE MERINGUE

Beat until foamy in a large bowl with an electric mixer
>6 EGG WHITES
>¾ TSP. CREAM OF TARTAR
>¼ TSP. VANILLA

Gradually drizzle in
>2-3 TBS. MILD FLAVORED HONEY (OR ¼ CUP MAPLE SYRUP)

Beat until whites are stiff and glossy.

*A sanded, unfinished board (a finish might burn) or any large pan (covered with foil or parchment paper to facilitate transfer of the BAKED ALASKA to a serving platter) may also be used.

ASSEMBLING THE BAKED ALASKA

Spread the meringue evenly over the ice cream cake, sealing it to the platter.**
Bake in a preheated 450° oven for 3-5 minutes, until lightly browned. Serve immediately.***

BAKED ALASKA has an infinite number of personalities. It can appear in many flavors and take on many shapes. Try molding the ice cream in a dome-shaped bowl, in 9" layer pans or in a free form log shape. Experiment with different cake/cookie bases as well as with different flavored ice creams.

**The meringue acts as insulation against the heat for the ice cream so spread and seal well!
***Baked Alaska may be frozen either before or after browning and served the next day. If browned ahead, return immediately to the freezer uncovered. Remove from the freezer 20-30 minutes before serving.

FROZEN SOFTIES

Delicious, spur-of-the-moment desserts, after-school snacks or Saturday afternoon refreshers can be whipped up in minutes in the food processor* when frozen milk or kefir cubes are kept handy in the freezer. Use the following recipes as is or elaborate and make them uniquely your own.

FROZEN SOFTIES can be made ahead and stored in the freezer. Let them sit at room temperature 15-30 minutes before serving.

The frozen cubes called for in the following recipes are from an average sized ice tray—about 2 tablespoons per cube.

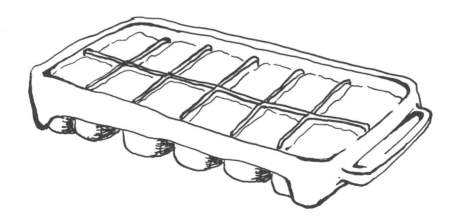

*Many blenders can handle FROZEN SOFTIES. All blenders have a preferred liquid-to-frozen ingredient ratio. Unlock the secrets of your blender and enjoy homemade softies often.

MAPLE DELIGHT

See page 102.

Remove from the freezer

> 1 ICE TRAY OF WHOLE MILK CUBES (ORIGINALLY 2 CUPS LIQUID)
>
> 4-6 FROZEN WHIPPED CREAM DOLLOPS*

Let sit for 5 minutes.

Combine in a food processor equipped with a chopping blade

> THE MILK CUBES, BROKEN IN 3-4 PIECES WITH A KNIFE POINT**
>
> THE DOLLOPS, CUT IN 3-4 PIECES EACH
>
> ½ TSP. VANILLA
>
> ¼-⅓ CUP REAL MAPLE SYRUP

Process, using on-and-off bursts at first. Then process continuously until velvety.

Spoon into 4-6 stemmed glasses.

*See page 124.

**Try breaking the cubes right in the ice tray before ejecting them.

BERRY SPOONER

See page 102.

Combine in a food processor equipped with a chopping blade

 HALF AN ICE TRAY (8 CUBES) OF WHOLE MILK CUBES*,
  BROKEN IN 3-4 PIECES WITH A KNIFE POINT**
 8 OZ. (½ LB.) FROZEN BLACK OR BOYSENBERRIES
 ¼ CUP BROWN SUGAR

Let sit for 5 minutes.

Process, using on-and-off bursts, to break up the berries and cube pieces.

Add

 ½ CUP MILK*
 ½ TSP. VANILLA
 1 TBS. LEMON JUICE

Process, using on-and-off bursts at first. Then process continuously until smooth.

Spoon into 4-6 stemmed glasses.

*Substitute buttermilk for a tangy variation.
**Try breaking the cubes right in the ice tray before ejecting them.

KEFIR SOFTIE

See page 102.
Combine in a food processor equipped with a chopping blade
  4 OZ. (¼ LB.) FROZEN WHOLE STRAWBERRIES
  6 CUBES FROZEN STRAWBERRY KEFIR*, BROKEN IN 3-4
    PIECES WITH A KNIFE POINT**
Let sit for 5 minutes.
Process, using on-and-off bursts to break up the berries and cube pieces.
Add
  ½ CUP BUTTERMILK
  2 TBS. BROWN SUGAR
Process, using on-and-off bursts at first.
Then process continuously
until smooth.
Spoon into 4-6 stemmed glasses.

*Kefir is a milk product similar to yogurt in nutrients, flavor and history. In contrast to yogurt, it is usually sold in liquid form and served as a tangy, fruit-flavored drink. Look for kefir in natural foods stores.

**Try breaking the cubes right in the ice tray before ejecting them.

MOM'S MAPLE BRAN MUFFINS

Combine in a large bowl
> 1 CUP UNPROCESSED BRAN
> 1 CUP MILK

Let stand until the bran absorbs most of the milk—about 3 minutes.
While the bran is soaking,
Mix well in a medium-sized bowl
> 1½ CUPS WHOLE WHEAT PASTRY FLOUR
> 2 TSP. BAKING POWDER

Set aside.
Add to the softened bran
> 2 EGGS
> ½ CUP MAPLE SYRUP
> ¼ CUP OIL
> ½ TSP. SALT

Beat well.
Add
> THE FLOUR MIXTURE

Stir just until combined.
Spoon into a buttered muffin tin.
Bake at 400° (preheated) for 20 minutes, or until golden brown.
Makes 12 muffins.
Serve warm with Mapley Butter.

MAPLEY BUTTER   .

Blend well in a small container with a lid
> 8 TBS. (ONE CUBE) BUTTER, SOFTENED
> 2 TBS. MAPLE SYRUP

Keep in the refrigerator.

OATMEAL DATE MUFFINS

Measure into a small bowl
    1 CUP DRY OATMEAL

Pour over the oatmeal
    ½ CUP BOILING WATER
Set aside to cool.

Mix in a large bowl
    ¼ CUP OIL
    ½-⅔ CUP BROWN SUGAR
    3 EGGS
    1 TSP. VANILLA
    ½ TSP. SALT
    1 TSP. BAKING SODA
    1½ CUPS WHOLE WHEAT PASTRY FLOUR*

Add and mix again
    ⅔-1 CUP (4-6 OZ.) MOIST CHOPPED DATES
    THE COOLED OAT MIXTURE

Spoon into a buttered muffin tin.
Bake at 350° for 20-30 minutes—until golden brown.
Makes 12 muffins.

*See page 124.

SCRUMPTIOUS GINGERBREAD PEOPLE

Blend well in a large bowl with an electric mixer
    ½ CUP SWEET BUTTER (SWEET = UNSALTED)
    1⅓ CUPS UNSULPHURED SWEET MOLASSES (GRAMMA'S
       IS ONE NAME BRAND)
    2 TSP. *EACH* GINGER, CLOVES AND
       BAKING SODA
    1 TSP. CINNAMON
    ½ TSP. SALT

Add, one cup at a time, blending after each addition
    4 CUPS WHOLE WHEAT PASTRY FLOUR*
Chill dough thoroughly.

Roll out on a floured cloth or board.
Cut into desired shapes.

Bake at 325° for 12-15 minutes.
Makes 4-5 dozen regular-sized cookies.

*See page 124.

Make GINGERBREAD PEOPLE on Halloween. They'll spring from the oven toasty-warm and mouth wateringly delicious in almost any size—from the tiniest minimen to 12" giants. Decorating giants is lots of fun for kids of all ages.

NANA BREAD

Mix well in a medium-sized bowl
>2 CUPS WHOLE WHEAT PASTRY FLOUR*
>1 TSP. BAKING SODA

Set aside.

Cream in a large bowl with an electric mixer
>½ CUP (ONE STICK) BUTTER
>1½ CUPS BROWN SUGAR

Add
>1½ CUPS MASHED VERY RIPE BANANA
>2 EGGS
>¼ TSP. SALT (½ TSP. IF BUTTER USED IS UNSALTED)
>1 TSP. VANILLA
>¼ CUP YOGURT

Mix well.

Add
>THE FLOUR MIXTURE
>½ CUP CHOPPED WALNUTS

Mix well.

Turn into a buttered and floured 9" x 5" bread pan.
Bake at 350° for 70-80 minutes—until a toothpick inserted in the center comes out clean.

*See page 124.

MARG'S ZUCCHINI BREAD

Mix well in a medium-sized bowl
> 1½ CUPS WHOLE WHEAT PASTRY FLOUR*
> ½ TSP. BAKING SODA
> ⅛ TSP. BAKING POWDER

Set aside.

Mix in a large bowl with an electric mixer
> 1 CUP BROWN SUGAR
> ½ TSP. *EACH* SALT AND CINNAMON
> 2 EGGS
> ⅓ CUP OIL
> 1½ TSP. VANILLA

Add
> THE FLOUR MIXTURE
> 1½-2 CUPS GRATED ZUCCHINI (2 CUPS MAKES A VERY MOIST BREAD)
> ½ CUP NUTS (OPTIONAL)

Mix well.

Turn into a buttered and floured 9" x 5" bread pan.
Bake at 350° for 60 minutes, or until a toothpick inserted in the center comes out clean.

Cool for 15 minutes and turn out onto a rack.
This is an easy recipe to double. It also freezes well.

*See page 124.

PIONEER PERSIMMON CAKE

Measure into a small bowl
> 1 CUP PERSIMMON PULP*
> 1½ TSP. BAKING SODA

Mix well.

Set aside.

Mix in a large bowl with an electric mixer
> ½ CUP BROWN SUGAR
> 3 TBS. BUTTER
> 1 EGG
> ¼ TSP. *EACH* SALT AND CLOVES
> ½ TSP. NUTMEG
> 1 TSP. CINNAMON

Add
> 1 CUP WHOLE WHEAT PASTRY FLOUR**
> THE PERSIMMON PULP (WHICH HAS GELLED!)

Mix well.

Stir in
> ½ CUP CHOPPED NUTS
> ¾ CUP RAISINS (OPTIONAL)

Turn into a buttered 9" x 9" pan.

Bake at 350° for 30 minutes, or until a toothpick inserted in the center comes out clean.

This cake keeps very well. Try making a double or triple recipe. Bake in small buttered pans and take as gifts on holiday visits.

---

*Use very ripe persimmons for this recipe. Wash and dry them while they are still firm. Put them in a brown bag with an apple. Close the bag and put it in a cool, dark cupboard. When the persimmons are very soft, remove the crowns. Tear or cut in half. Remove and discard the seeds (if any). Blend in a blender until smooth.

**See page 124.

CAROB CAKE

Mix in a large bowl with an electric mixer
    1½ CUPS BROWN SUGAR
    ¾ CUP OIL
    3 EGGS
    1 TSP. VANILLA
    ½ CUP CAROB POWDER (SCANT)
    ½ TSP. SALT

Combine in another large bowl
    2¼ CUPS WHOLE WHEAT PASTRY FLOUR* (SCANT)
    1 TSP. *EACH* BAKING POWDER AND
      BAKING SODA
Mix well with a fork.

Add to the carob mixture
    1 CUP WATER
    THE FLOUR MIXTURE
Mix well.

Turn into 2 buttered 9″ layer pans or one 9″ x 13″ loaf pan.
Bake at 350° for 25-30 minutes in the layer pans or 35-40 minutes in the loaf pan.

*See page 124.

SEASONAL MENU

SUGGESTIONS

SPRING

MEXICAN FIESTA

HIGH PROTEIN ENCHILADAS, page 22

LARGE GREEN SALAD

FIESTA FRUIT PLATTER

Slices of   Melon
                       Pineapple
                       Mango
                       Papaya
Sprinkled with Grated Coconut
                       Toasted Almond Bits

FINGER PICNIC

LEAPIN' LENTILS, page 33

LARGE LETTUCE LEAVES and GREEN PEPPER HALVES
STEAMY ROLLS
or
PITA BREAD HALVES and a VEGETABLE GARNISH PLATTER*

CORN-ON-THE-COB and/or DEVILED EGGS, page 84

CAROB CAKE SQUARES with ORANGE SECTIONS, page 113

*Offer shredded lettuce, cherry tomato halves and alfalfa sprouts to garnish the lentils
in the pita bread halves.

BUENA COMIDA

STACK-A-TORTILLA*, page 41

CUSTARD GARNISHED WITH ORANGE SECTIONS

EASTER BRUNCH

Start a new tradition. Gather with friends for a late morning egg hunt
and make your main Easter meal a leisurely brunch.

STEMMED GLASSES BRIMMING WITH SPARKLING APPLE JUICE
GARNISHED WITH WHOLE STRAWBERRIES

OVEN OMELETTE, page 17

Choose from   OATMEAL DATE MUFFINS, page 107
NANA BREAD, page 110
ZUCCHINI BREAD, page 111
MOM'S MAPLE BRAN MUFFINS, page 106
Spread with   MAPLEY BUTTER, page 106
CRUNCHY CREAM CHEESE SPREAD, page 87
SWEET PEANUT BUTTER SPREAD, page 86

FRUIT SALAD**and CREAMY DRESSING, page 92

*How about a standing ovation for the tallest or most beautiful stacked tortilla—and a booby prize for the most unstable?
**Combine chunks of apples, oranges, and bananas. Toss with currants and coarsely chopped nuts. Garnish with spring strawberries if possible. Offer the dressing on the side.

SUMMER

SIMPLE SUMMER SPREAD

CRUSTLESS QUICHE, page 18

SLICED TOMATOES DRIZZLED WITH
OIL AND VINEGAR DRESSING

CORN-ON-THE-COB

ICE CREAM CAKE

EASTERN ELEGANCE—EASILY

WON-TON HORS D' OEUVRES*

SHABU-SHABU TERADA, page 30

GREEN TEA and/or SAKE

SHORTCAKE WITH SLICED PEACHES AND FRESH BLUEBERRIES
or
MANDARIN YOGURT WITH A SPRINKLE OF CHOPPED WALNUTS
and/or
JAPANESE PLUM WINE

*Available in market frozen food sections.

LENTIL FEAST

LENTIL BOWLADO, page 35

ICE CREAM and NANA BREAD, page 110

INDEPENDENCE DAY FETE

SUMMER FRUIT SALAD, page 70

CALIFORNIA PINTO PLATTER, page 44
or
ELLIOT'S BLACK BEAN EXTRAVAGANZA, page 45

Offer bowls of   Natural Corn Chips
Don's Guacamole, page 82
Sour Cream
Chopped Green Onions
Chili Salsa

MAKE-YOUR-OWN-SUNDAES, page 99

MAKE-YOUR-OWN-SALAD-PICNIC

SALAD SPECTACULAR, page 76

WHOLE GRAIN ROLLS

BAKED ALASKA, page 100

FALL

MAKE-YOUR-OWN-SANDWICH DINNER

Set a spread—3 or 4 breads, 4 or 5 fillings, condiments and toppings. Let everyone create his own appetite satisfier. With a cool cup of soup and an eye to the easy lunches and snacks that can follow from your original efforts, MAKE-YOUR-OWN-SANDWICH DINNER is a winning fall theme—on the patio or in the dining room.

CHILLED GAZPACHO, page 61

Choose from   Warmed Chapatis, Tortillas, or Pocket Bread
Large Crackers
Whole Grain Breads

Fill with   Abby's Sandwich Filling, page 10
Surprise Loaf, page 49
Encore Dips, page 83
Tofu Mexicano, page 14
Crunchy Cream Cheese Spread, page 87
Sweet Peanut Butter Spread, page 86

Top with   Sprouts
Avocado Slices
Lettuce Leaves
Tomato Rounds
Pickle Slices
Cheese Slices

YOGURT CREAM PIE, page 96

PICK-A-PIZZA PICNIC

PIZZA OLÉ , page 38
or
ITALIAN-STYLE VEGETARIAN PIZZA, page 37

LARGE GREEN SALAD

FROZEN SOFTIES, page 102

FONDUE PICNIC

FAMILY FONDUE (without chiles), page 11

SWEET SPINACH SALAD, page 74

APPLE DELIGHT, page 94

THANKSGIVING FEAST

THANKSGIVING PUMPKIN SOUP, page 66

CORNBREAD and CRANBERRY SAUCE

A LONG WALK

PIONEER PERSIMMON CAKE, page 112

WINTER

RAINY DAY PICNIC

MEXICAN EGGPLANT, page 24

LARGE GREEN SALAD or BAKED SQUASH, page 60

PEARS and SCRUMPTIOUS GINGERBREAD PEOPLE, page 108

ROUND-THE-HEARTH BUFFET

POTATO CRUST QUICHE, page 26

STEAMED PEAS and CARROTS

ELEGANT WINTER FRUIT DESSERT, page 91

WINTER WARMER

SPLIT PEA SOUP, page 65

CORNBREAD

BAKED APPLES, page 95

WINTER SOUP SUPPER

GLORIA'S LENTIL SOUP, page 64

STEAMY ROLLS

PUMPKIN PUDDING, page 98

ARABIAN NIGHT

ARABIAN TACOS, page 48

RATATOUILLE* and/or SIMPLY BROILED MUSHROOMS, page 52

WINTER FRUIT and CHEESE BOARD

Offer Grapes
             Pears
             Apples
With   Gjetost
             Bonbel or Bel Paese
             English Chesire or
             a Good White Cheddar

*Ratatouille is a mixture of sautéed onions, tomatoes, zucchini, and eggplant cubes (possibly carrot and celery chunks) simmered until tender. It's delicious hot or cold.

APPENDIX

EXTRA WHIPPED CREAM? Spoon the whipped cream onto a plate in serving-sized dollops and pop into the freezer. When the dollops are firmly frozen, transfer them to a cold container and return quickly to the freezer. (Letting the plate sit several seconds at room temperature before removing the dollops with a thin spatula makes the job easy.) Frozen dollops thaw in about 20-30 minutes and can be used to make ordinary drinks and desserts something special.

EXTRA LEMONS? If you are fortunate enough to have a lemon tree—or know a generous neighbor with one—make some room in your freezer. Lemons can be washed, dried, and frozen whole in plastic bags or other freezer containers. The rind or juice can be readied anytime at a few moments notice. Lemons grate beautifully right from the freezer (wear a glove if your hand is temperature sensitive). Grate immediately and return to the freezer. To juice a frozen lemon immerse it in about a quart of water for a few minutes. Juicing it while it is still partially frozen expedites the thawing of the juice crystals. Refreeze extra juice in an ice cube tray.

WHOLE WHEAT PASTRY FLOUR? Whole wheat pastry flour has less gluten than whole wheat bread flour (often just called whole wheat flour) and makes a lighter, more tender product. If you like less chewy quick breads, cakes and cookies, choose pastry flour for these recipes. Do not use pastry flour when making yeast breads, however. Its lower gluten content will not allow the bread to rise properly.

The best place to store whole wheat flours is in the freezer. They must be well wrapped so they do not absorb moisture. If you cannot freeze your flour supply, buy only as much as you will use in three or four weeks and store, tightly wrapped, in the refrigerator.

TO COOK BEANS   Beans need to be rinsed and sorted before cooking to remove field dust, pebbles and bad beans.

There are several ways to cook beans. The simplest is to bring them to a boil in a pot of water (3-4 times as much water as beans) and simmer until tender. The pot will probably boil over if it is completely covered, so leave a little space for steam to escape. Check the beans occasionally and add water as necessary to keep them covered. Methods to shorten the cooking time include

1) THE OVERNIGHT SOAK—refrigerate the beans overnight in 3 cups of water for each 1 cup of beans. The next day, drain the beans and cook as above.

2) THE HOT, HOUR SOAK—hold unsoaked beans and water at a rolling boil for fifteen seconds. Cover, remove from heat, and let sit for one hour. Then cook as above.

3) THE PRESSURE COOKER—eliminate soaking and cut bean cooking time almost in half. Cook all *whole* beans (except for lima, black, and soy, which tend to foam and may clog the vent) more quickly in the pressure cooker.

Cooking times vary not only among different types of beans, but also among different aged beans of the same kind. Old beans take longer to cook than young ones so suggested cooking times are always approximations. A good rule of thumb is to cook the beans for the length of time suggested and then sample a few. If the beans are to be served whole (as in a salad) cook until evenly tender throughout. If the beans are to be mashed, cook until very soft.

Cooking beans is a long, but easy process. Cook extra beans whenever possible. Extras keep in the refrigerator for a week or can be frozen for longer periods. With cooked beans on hand, soups, tostadas, enchiladas, and stews are just a half-hour away.

INDEX

Other FRESH PRESS Books

THE BUSY PEOPLE'S NATURALLY NUTRITIOUS DECIDEDLY
DELICIOUS FAST FOODBOOK

TOFU GOES WEST

TOFU AT CENTER STAGE